Conflict, People & Power

Medieval Britain 1066–1500

FOUNDATION

JOHN D. CLARE

HISTORY

Hodder & Stoughton

A MEMBER OF THE HODDER HEADLINE GROUP

Acknowledgements

The front cover shows the Battle of Agincourt reproduced courtesy of ET Archives, and Henry V reproduced courtesy of The Bridgeman Art Library.

The publishers would like to thank the following individuals, institutions and companies for permission to reproduce copyright illustrations in this book:

Aerofilms Limited p14 (top), 15 (bottom); Ancient Art & Architecture Collection Ltd p52; The Ashmolean, Oxford p7 (left); The Bodleian Library p25, 49 (right); The Bridgeman Art Library p2, 4, 5 (both), 30, 63; The British Library p20, 33, 35, 39 (all), 48, 49 (left), 51 (top); The British Museum p7 (right); King's College Foundation Charter, Cambridge University Library p19; Corbis p14 (bottom); Corpus Christi College, Cambridge p17; English Heritage Photographic Library p15 (top left) (Andrew Tryner), 36 (© Crown Copyright. NMR), 42, 43, 46; e.t. archive, Musee de l'Assistance Publique p50; Hulton Getty p53; A.F. Kersting p 13; Life File/Nigel Shuttleworth p31; The Royal Library, Windsor Castle p9; The Marquis of Salisbury p45; The National Museums & Galleries of Wales p58; The Wellcome Institute Library, London p51 (bottom); Welsh Historic Monuments/T Ball p15 (right).

The publishers would also like to thank the following for permission to reproduce material in this book:

Blackwell Publishers for the extract from *Economic History Review*, Vol L1, No. 2, May 1998 by M Bailey and for the extract from *Peasant Life in the Medieval West* by R Fossier, 1988; Boydel & Brewer Ltd for the extracts from *The Normans and the Norman Conquest* by R Allen Brown, 1985; Cambridge University Press for the extracts from *Medieval Women* by E Power, 1975, and *The Agrarian History of England and Wales* 2, 1942-1350 by H E Hallam, 1988; Curtis Brown on behalf of Philip Ziegler for the extracts from *The Black Death* copyright © Philip Ziegler, 1982; Extracts from *Anglo-Saxon Chronicle*, edited by GN Garmonsway, 1972, reprinted by permission of Everyman Publishers PLC; ITPS Ltd for extracts from *The Fourth Estate* by S Shahar, 1983; Macmillan Press Ltd for the extracts from *The Making of Britain: The Middle Ages*, (ed.) L Smith, 1985; The extracts from *The Revolt of Owain Glyndwr* by R R Davies, 1995, have been adapted by permission of Oxford University Press; The extract from *Magna Carta* (Introduction by D Stroud), published 1980, by Paul Cave Publications Ltd; Phoenix House for the extract from *Medieval Women* by H Leyser, 1995; Extracts from *Life in a Monastery*, 1998 © Pitkin Unichrome Ltd by Stephen Hebron; Sutton Publishing for extracts from *Military Campaigns of the Wars of the Roses* by P Haigh, 1995 and *New Towns of the Middle Ages* by M Berisford, 1988; Weidenfeld and Nicolson for the extract from *Ireland* by R Kee, 1980.

Comic strip p22 from *Horrible Histories: The Measly Middle Ages*, text © Terry Deary, 1996, Illustrations © Martin Brown 1996, first published by Scholastic Ltd.

Please note that all sources have been adapted to make them more accessible to students.

Every effort has been made to trace and acknowledge ownership of copyright. The publishers will be glad to make suitable arrangements with any copyright holders whom it has not been possible to contact.

Orders: please contact Bookpoint Ltd, 78 Milton Park, Abingdon, Oxon OX14 4TD. Telephone: (44) 01235 827720, Fax: (44) 01235 400454. Lines are open from 9.00 - 6.00, Monday to Saturday, with a 24 hour message answering service. Email address: orders@bookpoint.co.uk

British Library Cataloguing in Publication Data
A catalogue record for this title is available from The British Library

ISBN 0 340 73046 3

First published 2000
Impression number   10 9 8 7 6 5 4 3 2 1
Year   2005 2004 2003 2002 2001 2000

Typeset by Liz Rowe.
Printed in Italy for Hodder & Stoughton Educational, a division of Hodder Headline Plc, 338 Euston Road, London NW1 3BH by Poligrafico Dehoniano, Italy.

Contents

IN THIS CHAPTER YOU WILL LEARN:

- **THREE** men who wanted to be king in 1066;
- **FIVE** reasons Harold lost the battle of Hastings;
- **FOUR** ways England changed after 1066.

NEW WORDS

army, battle, fight, died, killed

King Edward

Harold Godwinson

Harald Hardrada, king of Norway

William of Normandy

THE BIG PICTURE

Four kings and two battles

On 5 January 1066, old King Edward died. Harold Godwinson became the new king of England. But two other men wanted to be king
5   of England . . .

First, Harald Hardrada came with an army. Harold Godwinson went to fight him. There was a battle. Harald Hardrada was killed. Soon after, William of Normandy came with a
10 bigger army. Harold Godwinson went to fight William.

There was another battle. This time, Harold Godwinson was killed. William became king of England.

Today, Normandy is part of France. In 1066, it was a separate country, with its own ruler – William of Normandy.

SOURCE **A**

◄It is January 1066. Harold becomes king of England. But the people see the star, and they are afraid about what is going to happen.

When William first landed in England, he tripped and fell. He laughed it off, saying, 'See – I have England in my hands now!'

I should be king!

Harold Godwinson   *Harald Hardrada*   *William of Normandy.*

All three men said they had a right to be king of England.
These pictures tell you why.

Tasks

1. Count how many times the words **army**, **battle**, **fight**, **died** and **killed** are used on page 2.

2. Copy – or make up – sentences about 1066 using these words.

3. What kind of a year was 1066?

4. Why did each man think HE should be king?

5. Who do YOU think should have been king?

3

The Battle of Hastings

Godwinson got his army ready

Harold Godwinson knew he would have to fight to be king.   He got his army ready.   He waited in London.   Nothing happened, so he
5 sent his army home.

Godwinson won the Battle of Stamford Bridge

Then, on 20th September 1066, Hardrada came to the north of England.   Harold went north to
10 fight him.   He took only five days to get there.
There was a battle.   Harold Godwinson won.

William won the Battle of Hastings

On 27th September 1066, William came to
15 England.   Harold Godwinson went back to London.   He took only four days to get back. Then, on 13th October he made his men march 60 miles to Hastings.   They marched all day and all night.   They were tired.
20 On 14th October 1066, there was a battle. Harold Godwinson's army lost the battle.

William became king

On Christmas Day, 1066, William became king of England.

NEW WORDS

archers, won, pray, pretend
Stamford Bridge: in the north of England.
Hastings: on the south coast of England.
Normans: men from Normandy.
Bayeux Tapestry

SOURCE A

Harold got a big army, and went to fight William.

William surprised him before he was ready.

But Harold and his men still did well.

▲ *Written in 1066 by a man who liked Harold.*

SOURCE B

▲*The Bayeux Tapestry was made by Norman women soon after 1066.   In this picture, William's men, on horses, fight Harold's army, on foot.*

SOURCE C

▲ *This is a picture from the Bayeux Tapestry. Harold's army was on a hill. William's men pretended to run away. Harold's men ran down the hill after them. But it was a trick! William's men turned round and killed them.*

SOURCE D

William's men said he had been killed.

But he said,

'Look at me – I am here! There is no place to run – we must win, or die'.

▲ *Written by a Norman, soon after the battle. He knew men who were in the battle.*

SOURCE E

Some of the best men in England died at the battle of Stamford Bridge.

Harold still went to fight William – before many of his men had got there.

▲ *Written by an English writer, about 30 years after the battle.*

SOURCE G

▲ *William's army had many archers. This picture from the Bayeux Tapestry shows a man hit in the eye by an arrow.*

Harold's body was so badly cut up in the battle that nobody could find his body. The Normans had to ask his girlfriend to find the body.

SOURCE F

The night before the battle Harold's men were drinking and singing. The Normans prayed all night.

▲ *Written in 1125. This did not happen! (See lines 18–19!)*

Tasks

1. Read page 4. Copy the four headings onto slips of paper. Muddle them up, and sort them out into the right order. Copy them out neatly in the right order.

2. Do a piece of drama, to work out where Harold went in September–October 1066.

3. Read **Sources A–G**. Suggest FIVE reasons why Harold lost the Battle of Hastings.

4. Put the reasons in order of importance.

Alric's new life

Your Mission: to find out if 1066 was a bad thing for the people who lived in England.

Q Write these words on slips of paper. Put them into two piles, **'Rich'** and **'Poor'** – **power, free, slaves, greedy, sad, happy, better, worse**.

In 1066, William became king. What happened to the people who lived in England?
One man we know about was called Alric. Before 1066, he had some land. William gave
5 his land to a Norman.
Alric was sad about this.

SOURCE A

Castles
William was always building castles. He was a hard man. He took a lot of money and gold from his people. He was greedy. If a man took one of his deer, he put his eyes out! Rich people did not like him. Poor people were sad.
But William did not care.

▲ *Written by an English man in 1087 (the year William died). He did not like William.*
Alric lived near a Norman castle. When they began to build a new castle, the Normans often put it on top of English houses. They did not care.

SOURCE B

Churches
England belongs to the Normans. They build big churches in every place. These churches look nice and new, but many people say they liked the old ones.

▲ *Written by an English man in 1125.*

Against William the Conqueror.

'The lives of English people changed a lot. These were bad times for them.'

SOURCE C

Poorer
The English people became poorer.

The Normans took their land and power.

▲ *Written by a modern historian.*

SOURCE D

Talking French
It was a take-over!

It was a big change.

No important people used English any more.

The king and all the top people talked in French.

▲ *Written by a modern historian.*

For William the Conqueror.

'Not much changed, and some things got better!'

Lost freedom?
In some places, poor people lost their freedom. But in other places, slaves were set free.

▲ *Written by a modern historian.*

◄ *A pot from the time. Pots did not change. Alric could have used a pot like this before 1066, or after 1066.*

Pots

New Laws
King William had great power.

He made laws to stop bad men. But he was kind to people who loved God.

You could go anywhere, and no one would rob you.

▲ *Written by an English man in 1087 (the year William died).*

NEW WORDS

rich, power, freedom, slave, greedy, better, worse, castle, church, laws, penny

▲ *A penny from the time. Money did not change. Alric could have used this penny before 1066, or after 1066.*

Tasks

Onto 8 small slips of paper, copy out the titles of **Sources A–H**. Looking at the sources:

1. Put the slips into two piles – 'things that changed a lot', and 'things that changed a little'. How much did Alric's life change after 1066?

2. Now put them into – 'things that made Alric's life worse', and 'things that did not make it worse'. Was Alric's life *much* worse after 1066?

2 AFTER THE CONQUEST – KEEPING CONTROL

IN THIS CHAPTER YOU WILL LEARN:

- THREE problems William had 1066–1086;
- THREE ways William kept control in England;
- SIX things Domesday Book tells us;
- FIVE reasons castles changed, 1066–1485.

Q Imagine you are a Norman. There are 5000 of you. You are in a country of a million people who hate you. Where would you want to live?

William's problems

William was king, but he did not have control of England. He had three big problems:

1. The English people hated him;

5 **2.** Some English people rebelled;

3. William did not know anything about England.

William got control of England by doing three things:

10 **a.** He did a survey of all the country;

b. He put castles all over England;

c. When the English rebelled, he killed them.

William's wars

In 1069, the English rebelled. William went
15 round the north of England.

He killed the people. He burned their houses. He burned the food. Many English people died.

The first castles

William gave all the land in England to the
20 Normans who had come with him. They put castles on their land, to keep control of the English.

NEW WORDS

problem, control, hate

survey: find out facts about a place.

counties

Yorkshire

burned

wall

rebelled: went against the king.

government: the way a king rules over the country.

motte and bailey: a kind of castle.

SOURCE A

William did not change everything in England.

England had a good government and this helped William.

He kept the old counties (such as Yorkshire).

He got money in the same way as Harold.

He got an army in the same way as Harold.

▲ *Written by a modern historian.*

How to build a Motte and Bailey Castle

1. Get lots of English people;

2. Make them dig up a lot of earth and make it into a big hill (called the 'motte');

3. Make them get lots of wood;

4. Use the wood to build a small castle (called a 'keep') on top of the motte – go there if there is a war;

5. Make the English people get more wood;

6. Build another wooden wall round the bottom of the hill, to make a large 'bailey' – live there when you are not at war;

7. Make the English give you lots of food and money!

Tasks

1. Match William's problems (1–3) with the ways he kept control (a–c).

2. Page 8 tells us 18 things about William. Find them and write them down.

3. Read this page. Imagine you are a Saxon, forced to help a Norman lord build his castle. At each stage, 1–7, say what you would be thinking and feeling.

SOURCE B

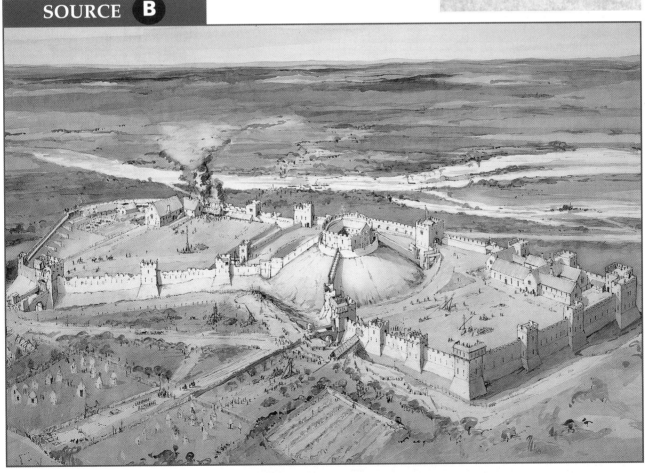

▲ *How is this castle better than most Norman 'Motte and Bailey' castles?*

THE BIG PICTURE

Q Imagine that friends from another country have come to visit you. They know nothing about where you live. List the SIX most important things you would tell them about your town.

NEW WORDS

wrote

worth

owned: to **possess**.

Domesday Book: a survey of England.

taxes: money you pay to the king.

reasons

Domesday Book

William needed money to fight all his wars. He wanted to get taxes from the people of England.

But how could he find out who should pay
5 what?

In 1086, he sent men all over England. In every place they wrote down:

1. how much land was there;
2. who had the land in 1066;
10 3. who owned it in 1086;
4. the kinds of people who lived there;
5. what the place was like;
6. what the land was worth in 1066 and 1086.

Domesday Book made William *very* powerful.
15 Now he knew everything about everywhere in England!

SOURCE A

William sent men all over England.

He told them to find out how much land there was, and what taxes he should get.

They wrote down all the land there was, and how much it was worth.

They wrote down how much land the king had, and how much land every man in England had.

Not one ox, cow or pig was left out.

It is bad to write about it – but William did not think it was bad to do it!

▲ *Written by an Englishman in 1086. He did not like William's survey.*

Tasks

1. Compare the six things the Domesday surveyors had to find out, with the list of things you said you would tell your friends. If the lists are different, suggest reasons why they are different.

2. Write out the letters: 'D-o-m-e-s-d-a-y-B-o-o-k' on 12 slips of paper. Muddle them up, then sort them out into the right order. Learn to spell 'Domesday Book'.

Looking at Domesday Book

Here are the people who lived in 1086 in a place in Yorkshire called Tanshelf.

One man wrote all Domesday Book! It has two million words and 13,418 places.

NEW WORDS

carucate: a lot of land (the same as 120 football fields).
burgess, cottager, miller, priest, smallholder, villager

I am Ilbert.
Tanshelf has 16 carucates of land. It was worth £20 in 1066, but it is only worth £15 now.

4th burgess:
King Edward used to own the place. Ilbert does now.

1st smallholder:
I have a little land. There are 8 smallholders like me.

1st burgess:
There are 60 burgesses in Tanshelf.

1st villager:
I am a farmer. There are 16 villagers in all.

2nd smallholder:
There is a small wood, where we get firewood.

2nd burgess:
There is a small field to grow grass for the cows.

2nd villager:
There is a place for fishing, down by the river.

1st cottager:
There are 16 cottagers. They are very poor.

priest:
I look after the church.

2nd cottager:
I do not own any land. I only have a little house.

3rd burgess:
We are important. We do not pay any taxes!

miller:
I am the miller. I own 3 mills!

3rd cottager:
There is some land for poor people, near the wood.

Tasks

Choose people in your class to be: Ilbert, burgesses, villagers, smallholders, cottagers, the priest and the miller. Ask your teacher to pretend to be the Domesday surveyor in 1086.

1. Answer the questions on page 10 as though you were there at the time.
2. Draw a picture of Tanshelf, showing everything that was there in 1086.

How and why did castles change?

a. Fire burned down wooden walls.

b. Attackers 'mined' under the walls.

c. After 1140, attackers invented new ways to capture a castle.

d. After 1270, people saw better castles in other countries.

e. After 1450, cannons were used.

Changes in Castles

Between 1066 and 1485 more than 1,500 castles were built! They got better and better as time went on.

The pictures on the left show 5
five reasons why castles changed.

1. Stone Castles

After 1085, people began to build *stone 'keeps'*, to stop attackers 10
burning down the walls.

2. Round Towers

After 1180, defenders built *round towers*, to stop attackers who tried to mine under the corners. 15

3. Curtain Walls

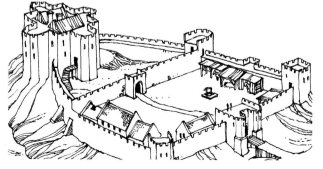

After 1200, defenders built a stone *'curtain wall'* around the bailey.

12

4. Even More Walls

20 After 1270, castles were built with two walls; (they were called '*concentric castles*'). And after 1300, buildings called '*barbicans*' were built to defend the gates (the weak part of a castle).

5. Manor Houses

25 But no castle wall could stop cannons. So after 1450 people went to live in '*manor houses*'.

Tasks

1. Find the SIX things in *italic* on pages 12–13. Write them out, learning how to spell them. Then write six sentences, about the words.

2. Use pages 12–13. Make a table with two columns. Copy the 'Reasons Castles Changed' (a–e) into the first column, and the 'Changes they caused' (1–5) into the second.

▲ *A barbican.*

THINKING IT THROUGH

▲ *A castle with a curtain wall.*

▲ *A keep (with a round tower).*

SOURCE D

▲ *A manor house.*

SOURCE E

▲ *A concentric castle.*

SOURCE F

People attacking a castle looked for a weak point. Many castles were captured when attackers climbed up the toilet chute!

◄ *A shell keep (made of stone).*

Tasks

1. Using the dates on pages 12–13, put the pictures in **Sources A–F** in order by date. Talk about the changes you see from one picture to the next.

2. Describe one of the pictures A–F in words. Can anybody guess which picture you are describing?

3. Find 10 words on pages 12–15 to do with castles. Work with a partner to learn how to spell them.

3 THE CHANGING POWER OF THE KING

IN THIS CHAPTER YOU WILL LEARN:
- TWO powerful and TWO weak kings;
- Parliament's FOUR 'steps to power';
- EIGHT facts about King John;
- FOUR things Magna Carta said.

Q Talk about the Royal Family. Do you like them? Do we need a Queen today?

If you wanted to be king . . .

. . . you had to be a man! There was only one queen in the Middle Ages, but there were 18 kings.

5 Kings were rich, and kings had power. But sometimes people rebelled. Five kings were killed.

Tasks

1. Look at Source A.
- Which TWO kings were powerful?
- Which TWO kings had little power?

2. Count the number of times the word 'war(s)' appears on this page. Count the number of times the word 'rebelled' appears. Now make up a sentence about kings in the Middle Ages using these two words 'wars' and 'rebelled'.

SOURCE **A**

Henry II, 1154–1189
Good in war. He built castles.

John, 1199–1216
He lost a war in France. He ran out of money. The barons rebelled.

Edward I, 1272–1307
He won wars in Scotland and Wales. He built castles.

Henry VI, 1422–1461 and 1470–1471. Mad. He lost a war in France. The barons rebelled and killed him.

▲ *Two strong and two weak kings.*

The power of the king

Three kings made the government better:

10 ● King Henry I set up a better way to get taxes and look after his money.

● King Henry II sent judges round the country, to make sure that people kept his laws.

● King John set up a better way of sending
15 letters to people, telling them what to do.

NEW WORDS

barons: rich lords.

queen, judges, crown, throne

orb: a gold ball, with a cross, a sign of kingship.

sceptre: a King's rod.

VI: 6th.

Laws were harsh in the Middle Ages. When some men took some money from Henry I, he cut off their right hands and their private parts!

SOURCE B

Churchmen put the crown on his head.

The 'orb' shows his power over people.

The 'sceptre' shows he makes the laws.

The barons say they will help him.

▲ *This is a picture of Edward III being crowned in 1327. Can you see the crown and the throne?*

Tasks

1. Look at **Source B**. Draw pictures of, and label, all the symbols of the king's power in the picture.

2. Copy from page 17 the three things that made the government better. Find and underline the words: laws, taxes and letters.

3. Use the information on pages 16–17 to make up a list of 'dos' and 'don'ts' advice for a medieval king.

Why did Parliament become important?

Q.
● Ask your French teacher what the French word 'parler' means.   Then work out what happens in 'Parliament'.
● What does the 'Speaker' always shout in the House of Commons?

NEW WORDS

Parliament: makes the laws which the people must obey.

MPs: Members of Parliament.

elect: to vote for.

commoners: ordinary people.

defeated

Speaker: the man elected by MPs to tell the king what they wanted.

wasted

strong

What is Parliament?

Today, we elect the Parliament.   And Parliament makes the laws we want.   This was not always so; at one time, the king had full power over the
5 country.
But slowly, Parliament grew in power.

How Parliament started

1. After 1066, the kings of England sometimes asked the barons to go to talk to them.

10 **2.** But, in 1258, the barons made Henry III meet them three times a year, even if he did not want to!   They called this meeting a 'parliament'.

3. Then, in 1264, the barons rebelled.   They
15 called another Parliament.   For the first time, they also asked 'commoners' to come to Parliament – two men elected from each county, and two from each town.
King Edward I defeated the barons, but he
20 still kept the Parliament – it was useful.   The king needed a lot money for his wars.   He got it from Parliament – Parliament let the kings take taxes.

SOURCE A

What are these bad men trying to do?

Do they think they are the kings of this land?

 ▲ *The king's brother said this in 1376, when Parliament would not give the king taxes.   What did he think about the Parliament?*

Until 1356, everybody spoke French in Parliament.   But in 1356, England was at war with France, so the MPs started to speak in English!

4. Slowly, Parliament grew more
25 powerful. In 1376, Edward III let
it elect a 'Speaker'. The Speaker
told the king what Parliament
wanted. The king did not like
being told what to do, but he
30 had to listen, because he needed
Parliament's money.

Parliament grew more
powerful. 300 years later, it was
strong enough to go to war with
35 the king. And it was the king
who lost that war.

SOURCE B

The king has asked us to give him
taxes. I think it is too much to give.

We have given so many taxes that
we have become weak.

The king has wasted all the money
we have given him.

▲ *This was what the first Speaker of
Parliament said in 1376. What did he think
about the king?*

SOURCE C

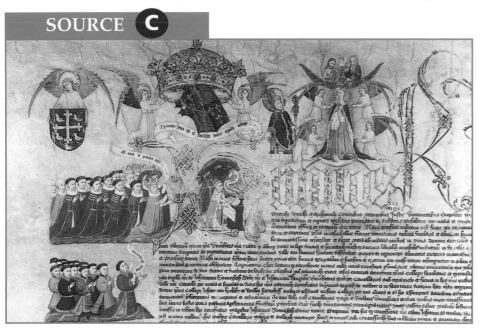

◄ *A drawing of Henry
VI and his Parliament.*

Tasks

1. Using pages 18–19, explain in your own words Parliament's 'FOUR
steps to power'.

2. Copy the following, choosing the right words:

Parliament's power **grue/grew/groo**.

It gave the king **tacks/taxis/taxes**.

Kings **needed/kneed/neaded** it.

Some MPs were **alected/elected/ilected**.

The Speaker told the king what Parliament **wonted/wantid/ wanted**.

'Bad King John'?

NEW WORDS

monk: a man who lives in a monastery.

enemies

wife

nephew

body

SOURCE A

▲ King John liked his dogs.

SOURCE B

King John had to judge a man who had killed a churchman.
  'Let him go', said John.   'He has killed one of my enemies.'

▲ Written by a monk.   King John fell out with the Church. This monk hated John.   Can we believe what he said?

King John 1199—1216 TIMELINE

1203: John killed his nephew, Arthur (who wanted to be king).

1204: John lost a war with France, and lost all his lands there.

1208: John fell out with the Church, but he had to give in.

1209: The King of Scotland was afraid of John.

1210: John won a war in Ireland.

1211: John won a war in Wales.

1214: John went to war with France, but lost.

1215: The English barons rebelled. John could not stop them.

SOURCE C

Everybody in Ireland, Scotland and Wales does what the king tells them to.

▲ *Written by a monk. This monk did not write many bad things about John. Can we believe what he said?*

SOURCE D

He had too much to drink, and killed his nephew Arthur with his own hands. Then he threw his body into the river.

▲ *Written by a monk. This monk was a friend of one of John's enemies. Can we believe what he said?*

SOURCE E

He was a bad king. He hurt his own people. He lost his lands in Normandy.
He hated his wife, and she hated him.

▲ *Written by a monk. King John fell out with the Church. This monk hated John too. Can we believe what he said?*

SOURCE F

John failed. But he was good at some things. He almost got back Normandy, and he almost defeated the English barons.
He made England stronger.

▲ *Written by a modern historian.*

SOURCE G

People were afraid of him. But he was a good king.

▲ *Written by a modern historian.*

Tasks

1. Copy the EIGHT facts on the timeline onto bits of paper (or photocopy and cut them up).

Sort them into two piles – one for John's successes, and one for his failures. Look at the facts in both piles.

● Are some facts more important than others?

● What do the facts show: was John a success or a failure?

2. Read **Sources A–E**.

● If we trust them, was John bad?

● Do you trust them?

3. Read **Sources F** and **G**.

What do they say: was John a success or a failure?

4. Discuss as a whole class:

Was King John a bad king, or a good one, a success, or a failure?

Was Magna Carta important?

Your Mission: to find out if Magna Carta was a waste of ink? Or was it the beginning of our freedom?

A Bad King!

King John fell out with one of the barons. He put the man's wife and son into prison.

All King John gave them to eat was a bit of
5 meat. Then he let them die. The mother died first. The boy started to eat the body of his mother before he died.

Magna Carta

Who knows if this story happened! People often
10 made up bad things about John.

But the barons hated John. They rebelled. In June 1215, they made John agree to Magna Carta – a long list of promises that the people of England would be free.

Q. ● List your own 'rights' (things that no one should stop you doing).

SOURCE B

Magna Carta – freedom under the law.

▲ *Written on a stone at the place where John agreed to Magna Carta.*

SOURCE C

King John hated Magna Carta.

The barons knew he was going to break his promises. They asked the king of France to send an army to help them fight the king.

Magna Carta was dead.

▲ *Written by a modern historian.*

SOURCE A

▲ *From a modern children's history book. It is just a joke.*

SOURCE D

King John made 63 promises in Magna Carta. These are the four most important:

All free men shall have these freedoms:

1. The Church shall be free;

2. The king will not take a tax unless Parliament agrees;

3. No free man shall be put in prison without a trial;

4. 25 barons will make sure that the king keeps his promises.

▲ *Think about these four promises, and try to explain why they are so very important.*
In 1215 most of the people in England were NOT free; they were owned by the barons! Magna Carta did not help ALL the people – just the rich people!

Tasks

1. What was Magna Carta (copy *lines 13–14*)?

2. Copy **Source D**.

3. Write sentences about Magna Carta containing each of these words: 'king', 'barons', 'promises', 'freedom' and 'prison'.

4. Read **Sources B–E**. Was Magna Carta important, or a waste of ink?

SOURCE E

Over the years, people forgot most of the promises in Magna Carta.

But as time went on, 'free men' came to be – not just the rich barons – but every man and woman in the country.

300 years later, when Parliament went to war with the king, people saw how important Magna Carta was.

And 500 years later, the people of America used its ideas when they rebelled against England.

▲ *Written by a modern historian. The Americans say all people have the right to have life and freedom, and to be happy.*

King John died in 1216 – of over-eating! He ate too many peaches and drank too much cider.

4 THE IMPACT OF CHRISTIANITY

IN THIS CHAPTER YOU WILL LEARN:

- 18 ways the Church in the Middle Ages was important to people;
- TWO kinds of monks in the Middle Ages;
- NINE things a nun had to do during the day.

Q. ● Do any of the class not believe in God? Share the different things you believe about God.

One God

In the Middle Ages, EVERYBODY in England believed in the same God – they were all *Christians*.
5   You could not believe in anything else.
In 1290 King Edward I made all the *Jews* leave England.

One Church

The Head of the Church was the *Pope*.   The
10 Church said that even kings had to do what the Pope said.
In England, the *Church* was run by the bishops and priests.
    The *bishops* went to Parliament and went to
15 war.   *Priests* looked after the churches.   They could read and write, so kings often asked them to help with the government.

Some Christians went on wars called 'crusades'.   They went to fight the Muslims – because they believed different things.   Even a king – King Richard I – went to fight in the Crusades.

NEW WORDS

Christians: believe in Jesus.

Jews: believe in God.

Muslims: believe in Allah.

Crusades: wars fought by Christians against Muslims.

Pope: Head of the Catholic Church.

bishop, prayers, drunk, wine

SOURCE A

We hate them, day and night.
    Their names will be taken out of the Book of Life.
And they will go to hell.

Λ *This was one of the Church's prayers.*
It was prayed about people who had said bad things about the Church.

The Power of the Church

Sometimes the king fell out with
20 the Church, but the Church was
very powerful.

The Church owned about ¼ of
the land in England. It had more
money than the king.
25 The Church had its own laws; the
king's judges could not send bad
priests to prison.

When King John fell out with the
Church, the Pope closed all the
30 churches in England for five years!

SOURCE C

A Bad Priest
He is a drunk, and sells wine to the
people so they get drunk too.

▲ *From a list of more than 50 bad priests,
made by a bishop.*

SOURCE B

▲ *People did as the Church said because
they were afraid of going to hell.*

Tasks

1. Find the SIX words in italics on
page 24. Write a sentence into
your book with each word in it.

2. Imagine you are a priest.
Using **Source B**, give a talk,
telling the people about hell!

3. 'Medieval Christians were not
very Christian!' Do you agree?

THE BIG PICTURE

Q. ● Imagine a pupil who is 'football mad'. How might football affect his life?

Everyday Lives

In the Middle Ages, the Church was very important in people's lives:

1. they went to church every Sunday;

2. every baby was baptised;

3. they got married at the church gate;

4. one in 50 people was a priest or a monk!

5. other people worked for the Church, such as builders;

6. the only holidays were Church Holy Days;

7. if they lost something, they prayed;

8. if they wanted something, they prayed;

9. workers said a prayer to make work go well;

10. if they wanted a book, a monk had to write it out by hand;

11. they went to a monastery to go to school – the monks were the teachers;

12. if they were going somewhere, a monastery was the only place to stay at night;

13. if they were ill, they went to a monastery – the monks looked after them;

14. if they were poor, they went to a monastery – the monks gave them food;

15. if a robber ran into a church, he could not be arrested;

16. crusaders went to fight for the Church;

17. just before they died, a priest gave them the last rites, so they would not go to hell;

18. when they died, the priest buried them.

NEW WORDS

baptised, married, buried, robber

arrested, traveller

holy: godly.

holidays

monastery: where monks live.

crusader: fights for the Church.

last rites: prayers for a dying person.

Medieval people believed that fairies would take a baby, putting a fairy-child in its place. If they thought this had happened, they would tie the baby to the roof, or put it in a hot oven!

The Impact of Christianity in the Middle Ages

1 Builder

2 Traveller

7 Crusader

4 Mother with a new baby

8 Student

3 Old woman

5 Priest

6 Ill man

Tasks

1. Play the memory game, 'I went to market . . .', saying instead 'I believed in God so I . . .'. Each player adds one more thing from the list on page 26.

How long can the class go on before you have to give up?

2. All the medieval people on this page are saying something about the importance of the Church in their lives – but the speech boxes have been left blank! Using page 26, suggest what each person may have been saying.

The Monk and the Robber

(this story was told by a French Bishop in about 1240.)

Once upon a time there was a bad man who robbed and killed many people. And there was a holy monk who heard what the man was doing. So, one day, the monk got on his horse
5 and went to the place where the robber lived.

When he saw the monk coming, the robber stopped him.

'What do you want?' asked the monk.

'Your horse and your clothes,' said the man.

10 'But I have had them a long time,' said the monk. 'Why do you want them?'

'Today I shall sell them to get bread and meat,' said the robber.

'Come back with me to the monastery,' said
15 the monk, 'and I will give you all you need.'

So the robber went back with the monk to the monastery, and there the monks gave him fine clothes, good food and a nice bed. He got everything he wanted. But the monks would eat
20 only bread and water.

After many days, the robber saw how much he had, and how little the monks had, so he asked one of the monks why this was so.

'Brother,' said the robber, 'you must have done
25 something very bad. Did you kill a man?'

'Not at all,' said the monk. 'I have never even got cross with another man.'

'Then why,' said the robber, 'do you have so little, and live such a poor life?'

30 'I live like this,' said the monk, 'to please God.'

When he heard this, the robber was very sad, and he said, 'I am a bad man. I have killed and robbed
35 – but this man has done nothing bad.'

And the robber fell at the monk's feet, and promised to change his life. He lived in the monastery, and became a monk.

NEW WORDS

story

magic

scared

knight

SOURCE A

A Bad Monk
He wanted money more than anything.
He tried to make money by magic, and took gold and things from the monks.

▲ *Written by a monk in about 1350.*

The Church told people that dances came from the devil! In one story, people danced in a church. On Sunday a thunderbolt killed them, and a devil came and took a bite out of the wall.

SOURCE B

▲ *People praying.*
In the Middle Ages, everybody believed in God – and hell.

Tasks

1. Tell the story, in turn, bit by bit, as a whole class.   Each person can add as little or as much as they want, but you must tell the whole story, and the last person must finish it off.

2. Working in pairs, devise and act out a dialogue to tell a part of the story.

3. Read **Sources A** and **C**.   What different impression to the story do they give about the way monks lived?   What TWO kinds of monks were there in the middle ages?

SOURCE C

A Bad Monastery
They do not pray.   They cannot sing.   They do not read books.   They do not love God.
   But they talk about bad things, and fight with each other.

▲ *Written by a monk in 1493.*

What was a nun's day like?

Your Mission: *to find what it was like to be a nun in 1200.*

NEW WORDS

worship
rules
punish
noon
Bible
statue
candles
stairs
sign language

Monks and nuns

Monks and nuns wanted to please God. They left their old life. They did not meet the other sex. They gave away everything they had and
5 promised to be poor. They worked hard. They prayed and worshipped God most of the day.

Q. ● Find THREE ways that a nun's life in the Middle Ages was different from yours today.

Many men and women became monks and nuns. By 1500 there were about 880 monasteries in England.
10 Why did people want to be monks and nuns?

SOURCE A

▲ *Nuns worshipping in about 1300, helped by some priests. List all the different things you can see in the picture which show they are in a church.*

SOURCE B

2 am: go to church.

4 am: read.

6 am: go to church.

9 am: go to church.

10 am: Chapter – go to hear the rules read out. Nuns who did not follow the rules were punished.

12 noon: go to church.

3 pm: go to church.

5 pm: go to church.

9 pm: go to church, then go to bed.

▲ *A nun's day in summer.*

SOURCE C

They do not wear fine clothes, and have no more clothes in winter. They sleep in their clothes, and do not go back to bed after they have gone to church at night.

They all go to church. They never leave the monastery. They do not speak.

They care for sick people, but take no care of themselves.

▲ *Written in about 1140.*

SOURCE D

They ate at about 11 am or 12 noon. A nun or a monk read to them from the Bible all the time they were eating.

They could not leave the table. They could not look around. They could not say anything.

To speak to each other, they used sign language. There were more than 100 signs for different kinds of food.

▲ *Written by a modern historian.*

SOURCE E

It was 3 am.

The church was full of nice smells.

A statue of Jesus was held up. We all went to it holding candles, and singing and praying.

▲ *Written by a monk.*

SOURCE F

▲ *Monks had to go to church at night. These stairs led from the church to their bedroom.*

Tasks

You are the Careers Officer for a convent.

1. Look at **Sources A–F**, and make up FIVE questions to ask people who want to be nuns.

Start your questions: 'Can you ...' or 'Do you like ...'. Ask a friend the questions. Would your friend make a good nun?

2. Write out on cards the NINE things that the nuns did during the day (**Source B**). Devise short mimes about what the cards say. Act them out, in order, to show 'A normal day' for a nun.

5 LIVING IN THE COUNTRY

IN THIS CHAPTER YOU WILL LEARN:

● **FOUR** kinds of people in Feudal England;
● **THREE** things a villein did for his lord;
● **FIVE** reasons the peasants revolted;
● **SIX** ways women had a hard life.

NEW WORDS

Feudal System

lord

strips

crops

villeins: peasants.

rents: money you pay for your land.

The Feudal System

King

When he became king in 1066, King William said that he owned all the land.

Barons

5 The king gave some land to his barons, if they promised to give him money and men for his army.

Knights

10 The barons gave some of their land to their knights, if they promised to fight for them.

Villeins

The knights gave a few strips of land to their villeins. For this, the villeins had to work on the 15 lord's land, hand over their crops, and pay money to the lord. The knight owned the villeins.

SOURCE A

Most people could not read or write. We know more about the rich than the poor.

▲ *Written by a modern historian. Most of what we know about the poor was written by the rich, and gives the lords' idea of the poor.*

I will give you some land –
you must send me men and money for my army.'

I will give you some land – you must fight for me in the king's army.

a. The baron gave me my land.

b. The knight gave me a few strips of land.

c. I work on my lord's land without pay.

d. I send knights to fight in the king's army.

e. My lord owns me.

f. Everything I have belongs to my lord.

g. I own ALL the land.

h. I cannot leave home – I am not free.

i. I give my lord most of my crops.

j. I must fight in the baron's army.

k. I do not own anything.

l. The king gave me my land.

SOURCE B

▲ *A peasant at work in about 1340. A villein's life was hard work.*

Tasks

1. Read sentences a–l on this page. Work out who would have said them – king, baron, knight or villein.

2. Find these words on pages 32–33:

king	leave	land	belongs
barons	free	knights	army
villeins	feudal	owns	crops
strips	work	give	money

3. Choose TEN words. Use each word to make up a sentence about the feudal system.

SOURCE C

They live in little huts, with too many children, and rents too high.

In winter – on cold nights without sleep – they get up when it is still dark to work.

They are hungry all day long.

▲ *Written by a poor priest about peasants, in 1390.*

I will give you some land – you must work for me and I will own you.

I do the work – they get all the money. What a life!

The Peasants' Revolt

Q. ● Have you ever been on a march or a protest?

Causes of the Peasants' Revolt

In 1381, the peasants rebelled.   There were FIVE reasons why they did so.

1. The King

5   Richard II was only 14 years old.

2. War

England was at war with France – and the war was going badly.   The government made a new tax – called a Poll Tax – to pay for the war.

10   ### 3. Bad lords

In 1348–51, the Black Death killed many people. There were not enough people left to work on the land.   Some lords tried to make the peasants work harder.

15   ### 4. John Ball

John Ball was a poor priest who did not like the rich lords.   He said that the lords should give their money to the poor.

5. Hate

20   The peasants hated being villeins.   They hated being poor and working for the rich lords.   They hated the Poll Tax and the war.

Task

Use the information on this page to write a sentence about each of the following:

- Richard II
- The Poll Tax
- The Black Death
- John Ball

SOURCE A

Rich people have big houses, while we have to work outside in the fields in the wind and the rain.

And if we do not work for them, they hit us.

We are like slaves.

▲ *John Ball said this to the peasants outside London in 1381.*

During the Revolt, the first thing many peasants did was to burn the houses of their lords.

SOURCE B

He said that poor people are as good as rich people.

When he said these mad things, they all loved him.

▲ *A monk wrote this about John Ball in 1381.   Peasants had just attacked his monastery, because it made them work for nothing.*

The Peasants' Revolt

In 1381, 30,000 peasants rebelled.   They asked
25 Wat Tyler to be their leader.   They went to
London.   They asked the king to set them free.

Richard II went to meet the peasants.   There
was a fight, and Wat Tyler was killed.

Richard II was brave.   'I will be your leader,'
30 he told the peasants, 'Go home.'   The peasants
went home.

After the Peasants' Revolt

Richard put many peasants to death.

'Villeins you were, and villeins you will stay',
35 he told them.

But the lords saw that things would have to
change.   They set their villeins free – 50 years
later, there were no more villeins in England.

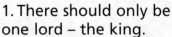

NEW WORDS

causes: reasons.
revolt: rebellion.
Poll Tax
Black Death: see
Chapter 7.
leader
brave

SOURCE D

1. There should only be
one lord – the king.
2. The Church should
give its money to help
poor people.
3. There should be no
more villeins: all men
should be free.

▲ *What the peasants asked
for in 1381.   This was written
by a monk.*

SOURCE C

▲ *This picture was drawn about 60 years after the Peasants'
Revolt.   On the left of the picture, Wat Tyler is killed.   On
the right of the picture King Richard tells the peasants to go
home.*

Tasks

1. Draw a
spidergram of the
FIVE causes of the
revolt.   Draw lines
between any that
are connected.

Which do you
think was the most
important cause?

2. Read **Source D**.
Draw a poster that
the peasants might
have carried in 1381.

3. Who won the
Peasants' Revolt?

The village vanishes

NEW WORDS

ruin

babies

village

century: a period of a hundred years.

bone

The old church stands alone. It is just a ruin now.

But once upon a
5 time there were people in it. Babies were baptised. Young people got married. Old people who died
10 were buried there.

Was there once a village round the church? Were there houses there? Did
15 children play there, and mothers clean and cook, and fathers work in the fields?

SOURCE A

▲ *The ruined church today.*

SOURCE B

Ansger has land there.

In King Edward's time the land belonged to Ailmer.

There is one slave and a farmer and a mill.

▲ *Written in Domesday Book, 1086.*

SOURCE C

Giles Brewosa, a knight, has this village.

His son John is three years old.

▲ *A tax survey, 1305.*

SOURCE D

Lord March has this land.

It used to belong to Giles Brewosa's family.

▲ *Tax surveys for 1399 and 1425.*

SOURCE E

The church was built in the 12th century.

Bits were added in the 15th century – a lot of people must have gone to the church at that time.

The church was being used in 1550, but not many people went there. Some people wanted to knock it down, but the bishop would not let them.

More people were going to the church in 1730, and some more bits were built on.

But then the roof fell in. People stopped going.

▲ *The story of the church, written by a modern historian.*

SOURCE F

Two farms. One garden. Some fields. A wood.

▲ *This is all that was left of the village in 1594.*

SOURCE G

1667 Sam and Mary.
1723 Richard.

▲ *The last babies baptised in the church.*

What there was in the field next to the church

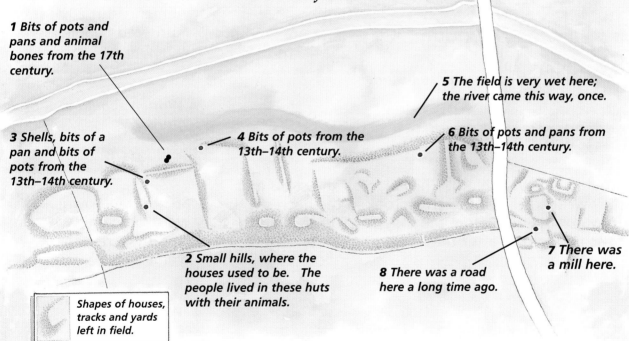

1 Bits of pots and pans and animal bones from the 17th century.

3 Shells, bits of a pan and bits of pots from the 13th–14th century.

4 Bits of pots from the 13th–14th century.

5 The field is very wet here; the river came this way, once.

6 Bits of pots and pans from the 13th–14th century.

2 Small hills, where the houses used to be. The people lived in these huts with their animals.

8 There was a road here a long time ago.

7 There was a mill here.

Shapes of houses, tracks and yards left in field.

Tasks

1. Who owned Knowlton in 1086?

2. When was the village biggest?

3. When did Knowlton disappear?

4. Use all the sources on pages 36 and 37 to work out FIVE things to say about what life was like in the old village of Knowlton.

History or Her-story?

Your Mission: to find SIX things that show that women had a hard life in the Middle Ages.

Woman are half our history – we should not just learn about 'his story', but we must learn about 'her story' as well!

Some historians think women were important
5 in the Middle Ages.   Some historians think that they had no power.   What do YOU think?

NEW WORDS

- protest
- murdered
- harvest
- wool
- husband
- servant
- beer
- cloth
- nurses
- blacksmith

SOURCE A

Sometimes there were women who were so powerful that they became leaders of the people.

In 1386, one woman led a village protest when the lord tried to make the people work harder.

▲ *Written by a modern woman historian.*

SOURCE B

Women did everything.   They planted the crops and they weeded the crops.   They took in the harvest. They got the wool from the sheep.   They milked the cows and looked after the hens.

▲ *Written by a modern woman historian.*

SOURCE C

She hears the children cry.   The cat eats the food and the dog eats the shoes.   Her bread burns on the fire, the cow drinks the milk and her husband gets cross.

▲ *A book from the Middle Ages, trying to get women to become nuns!*

SOURCE D

Only 8% of killers were women.   But 20% of murdered people were women.

▲ *Written about the 13th century.*

SOURCE E

86% of land-owners were men; only 14% of land-owners were women.

▲ *Written about the years 1350–1450.*

SOURCE F

The men worked in the fields or the wood.   The women did EVERYTHING else.

▲ *A modern historian says women were important.*

SOURCE G

▲ Pictures of people in about 1340.

SOURCE H

114 servants

100 made cloth

39 made beer

11 inn-keepers

2 nurses

2 farmers

3 blacksmiths

2 made shoes

1 shop-keeper.

▲ Some of the jobs done by women who had to pay tax in about 1385.

SOURCE I

They had no power.

When they got married, they lost most of their freedom.

Everything important in the home was done by their husband.

They just did all the dull jobs.

▲ A modern woman historian.

Tasks

1. Look at **Sources A–I**. Find some sources:

● which suggest women were important,

● which imply that men were more important.

2. Find SIX things which show that women had a hard life in the Middle Ages. Make up three 'laws' which would have made women's lives easier.

3. Imagine you are a medieval parent telling your daughter about a woman's life. What advice would you give her?

6 TOWNS IN THE MIDDLE AGES

IN THIS CHAPTER YOU WILL LEARN:
- FOUR ways towns changed;
- SIX reasons why towns became important;
- THREE good places to build a town.

Q
- Imagine a visit to a nearby town today. What can you do there?
- Look at this picture. How are towns today different from towns in the Middle Ages?
- Are they the same in any way?

NEW WORDS

charter: gave the townspeople rights – such as the right to hold a **market**.

craftsmen: they make things.

buy

merchants: rich **traders**.

Town Council: people elected to run a town.

Lord Mayor

perhaps

dirty

What do you think of when I say 'town'?

Wooden houses with large gardens behind.

It has a market.

It is run by the rich merchants and – sometimes – a Mayor.

It has a charter which gives the townspeople rights.

People do not have to work for a lord.

Craftsmen live there. They make and sell things.

Places to work.

Places to have fun.

Lots of people.

Lots of shops.

It has a Town Council.

Middle Ages

Today

SOURCE A

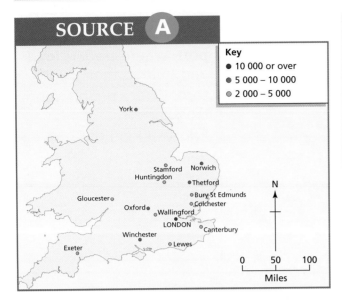

Key
- 10 000 or over
- 5 000 – 10 000
- 2 000 – 5 000

▲ *English towns in 1086.*

SOURCE B

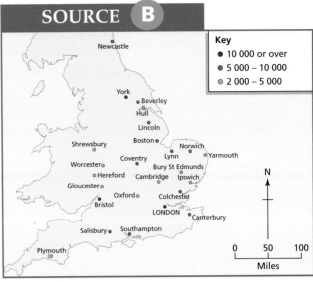

Key
- 10 000 or over
- 5 000 – 10 000
- 2 000 – 5 000

▲ *English towns in 1400.*

Q ● Act out, or tell, the story of Dick Whittington.

How Towns Changed

There really was a Dick Whittington! He lived in the 14th century. He went to live in London and became a rich merchant and the Lord Mayor
5 of London. Perhaps he had a cat – we will never know!

Dick Whittington was like many people in the Middle Ages who went to live in the towns. So towns changed; they grew bigger.
10 A second change was that there were more towns. In 1086 there were 111 towns in England. In 1370 there were 510.

Another way towns changed was that craftsmen set up workshops there. Merchants
15 and traders lived there, too. Like Dick Whittington, they went on ships and sold things all over the known world. Towns became places where these rich people lived.

A fourth change happened after 1400. Before
20 this, most town houses had been made of wood. After 1400, rich townspeople began to build their houses out of stone. Why was stone better than wood?

Tasks

1. Go round the class in turn. Each pupil reads out a sentence from pages 40–41 with the word 'town' in it. How long can you keep going?

2. Find FOUR ways towns changed in the Middle Ages. Write a sentence about each.

3. Work in twos. Imagine one of you lives in a town; your friend lives in the countryside. Try to persuade your friend to go to live in the town.

Totnes – A changing town

These two pictures show what Totnes may have looked like in 1100 (left) and in 1400 (right).

These are modern pictures, not pictures from the time.

SOURCE A

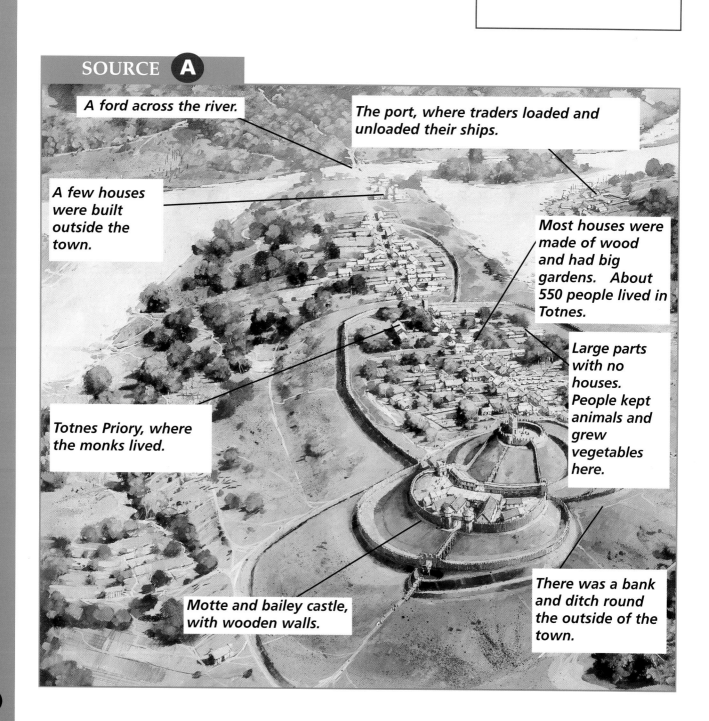

A ford across the river.

The port, where traders loaded and unloaded their ships.

A few houses were built outside the town.

Most houses were made of wood and had big gardens. About 550 people lived in Totnes.

Large parts with no houses. People kept animals and grew vegetables here.

Totnes Priory, where the monks lived.

Motte and bailey castle, with wooden walls.

There was a bank and ditch round the outside of the town.

Tasks

1. Look at the two pictures. Working as a whole class, list all the differences you can see between Totnes in 1100 and Totnes in 1400. Make a spidergram to record your answers.

2. Working as a whole class, write FOUR sentences about how Totnes changed. Mention:

- how big it was,
- new towns nearby,
- the port,
- buildings in the town.

SOURCE **B**

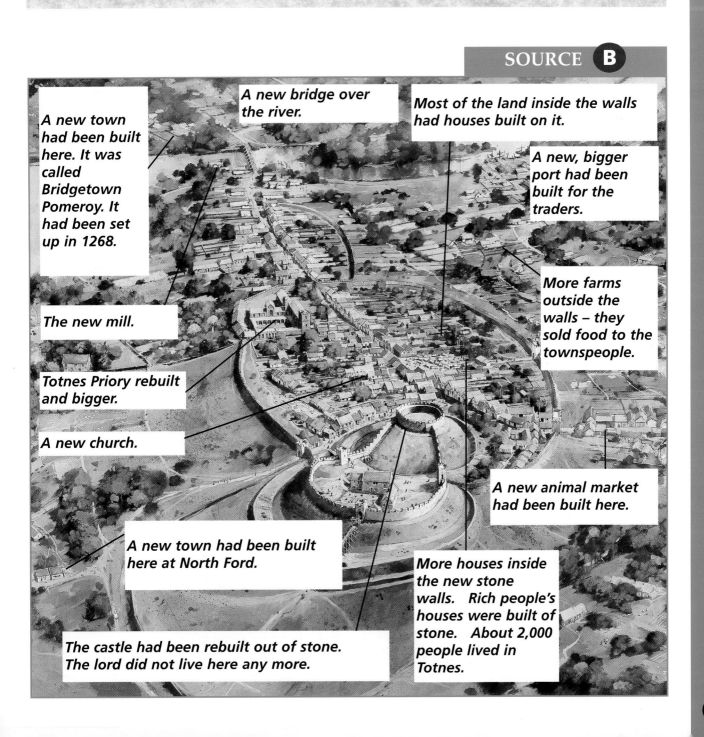

A new bridge over the river.

Most of the land inside the walls had houses built on it.

A new town had been built here. It was called Bridgetown Pomeroy. It had been set up in 1268.

A new, bigger port had been built for the traders.

More farms outside the walls – they sold food to the townspeople.

The new mill.

Totnes Priory rebuilt and bigger.

A new church.

A new animal market had been built here.

A new town had been built here at North Ford.

More houses inside the new stone walls. Rich people's houses were built of stone. About 2,000 people lived in Totnes.

The castle had been rebuilt out of stone. The lord did not live here any more.

Why did towns become important?

In 1297, England and Scotland were at war. In the same year, King Edward I gave orders to rebuild the town of Berwick.

Berwick is on the border between England and
5 Scotland. King Edward himself helped to build the town's new walls.

Q. ● Why was Berwick so important to Edward I?

Why Were Towns Important?

Towns were important in the Middle Ages because:

10 **1. Freedom**: Townspeople were free. The law said that a villein could become a free man if he lived in a town for a year and a day.

2. Law and Order: A few soldiers in a town could control the countryside round about.

15 **3. Money:** Lords could make money from towns. People gave them rent for some land, or for a market stall.

4. Trade: Traders lived in the towns.

20 **5. War:** Towns had walls which stopped attackers.

6. The King: Sometimes a town grew up near a place where the king stayed.

The town of Baldock, in the south of England, was named after Baghdad, the big city in modern Iraq! It hoped to become as rich and famous as the real Baghdad.

SOURCE A

The Bishop has built a row of houses in the middle of the market place, so that he will get more rent.

▲ *Written in 1279, about the town of New Thame.*

FREEDOM

LAW AND ORDER   MONEY

TRADE   WAR

THE KING

SOURCE B

▲ *A map of the town of Conwy in Wales. Find the castle and the town walls.*

SOURCE C

There are many robbers and bad men there. There is a plan to set up a town of merchants.

▲ *Written in 1324, about the town of Bala in Wales.*

SOURCE D

A man who lives there for a year and a day shall be free.

▲ *Written about 1200, in the charter for Haverford West.*

SOURCE E

They shall not have to pay any tolls wherever they go in the land or at the sea ports.

▲ *Written in 1142, about the merchants of Devizes.*

SOURCE F

The king's men lived too far from his hunting house. The king gave land to traders so that they would come and build a market town.

▲ *Written in 1279, about the town of New Woodstock.*

Tasks

1. Working as a whole class, discuss the six reasons why towns were important in the Middle Ages. Write out the six reasons on slips of paper.

2. Put the six reasons on page 44 into their order of importance – in your opinion.

3. Sources A–F are documents from the time.

Each one is an example of a reason why towns were important in the Middle Ages. Can you match the six reasons, 1–6, with the six sources, A–F?

On the move

Your Mission: to tell the Bishop where to put his 'new town'.

NEW WORDS

cathedral
chalk: a white rock.
valley
bully
blind
cost
exaggerating
desert

We Need A New Town!

It is 1218 – Richard Poore is Bishop of Salisbury. His cathedral is high on a hill called Old Sarum. Many people want him to build a new cathedral, with a new town around it – in a place where it can grow.

A good place to build a new town would be:
● at a place where roads meet (good for traders);
● by a river (good for water, and for ships);
● on land owned by the Bishop.

SOURCE A

Let us go down to the valley, where the fields are beautiful and where there is freedom.

▲ *Written by a Frenchman, in 1199.*

SOURCE C

1137: In this year the king put the Bishop in prison.

He kept him there until the Bishop gave his castle to him.

▲ *Written in 1137. It shows that Old Sarum was an important place.*

SOURCE B

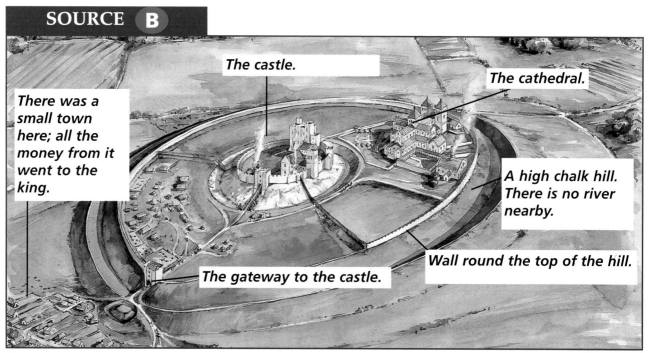

The castle.

The cathedral.

There was a small town here; all the money from it went to the king.

A high chalk hill. There is no river nearby.

Wall round the top of the hill.

The gateway to the castle.

▲ *A picture of the old town in 1130, before the Bishop set up the new town.*

SOURCE D

The soldiers in the castle bully us; they stop people going to visit the church.

The wind blows so loudly round the hill that we cannot hear each other sing. We catch cold. The church shakes with the winds.

Some of the priests have gone blind because of the sun which shines on the chalk.

We have to carry the water a long way and it costs a lot.

▲ *A letter to the Pope from a priest in 1217. He was asking the Pope to let them move, so he may be exaggerating – he wanted to make the place sound bad!*

SOURCE E

It was like a desert – no rain, flowers or grass. No birds sang. There was little water, and the climb to the top of the hill tired us out.

▲ *Written by a priest about 1218.*
He may be exaggerating – he wanted the Bishop to move the cathedral!

Tasks

Prepare a class drama. Your teacher will play Bishop Richard Poore. You will play his priests. You visit him and:

1. tell him all your problems.

2. persuade him that a move will solve your problems – and will help him.

3. choose a place on the map (1–5) to set up a new town. Show the Bishop how it is a good place to build a town (see page 46).

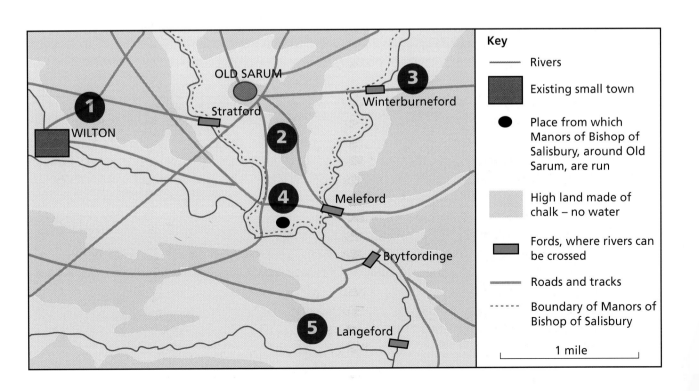

Key
— Rivers
■ Existing small town
● Place from which Manors of Bishop of Salisbury, around Old Sarum, are run
High land made of chalk – no water
▬ Fords, where rivers can be crossed
— Roads and tracks
---- Boundary of Manors of Bishop of Salisbury
1 mile

OLD SARUM
Stratford
Winterburneford
WILTON
Meleford
Brytfordinge
Langeford

THE BIG PICTURE

IN THIS CHAPTER YOU WILL LEARN:
- TWO reasons diseases spread;
- FOUR cures doctors used;
- FOUR ways medicine changed.

Q.
- How long do you want to live?
- What do people die from, nowadays?

Why did so many people die?
In the Middle Ages, most men died before they were 40 years old. Women died even younger – many women died having a baby.

5   Many people died if they became sick. Sometimes great plagues killed many people.

Why did diseases spread?
Traders went to far-away places, and came back with new diseases.

10   In the Middle Ages, no one knew that it is important to keep clean. Towns were very dirty places. Also people ate food that had gone bad – many people died from tummy bugs.

NEW WORDS

disease: an illness, when a person falls sick.

plague: a disease which kills lots of people.

spread

doctor: in the Middle Ages, almost always a man, who tried to make people better.

medicine: what you take to make you better.

operation: when a doctor cuts open the body to try to make the person better.

clean

pain

blood

A picture showing three people, and what they will become – three dead people. In the Middle Ages people thought that Death was all-powerful. They knew they would die young. ▶

SOURCE B

Traders went to far-away places. ➤

In London one man let all his toilet waste run into his cellar. One day, he fell through the floor – and drowned in it!

SOURCE C

An operation to help a mother have a baby (1375).

What did doctors do?

Doctors did not know the causes of disease, but they still tried to make people better. They cut sick people to take away 'bad' blood. They gave people medicines made from plants and things like frogs (some of these medicines killed the sick people)! Some doctors used magic. Everybody said you could get better if you prayed to God.

Most people died after an operation. There was nothing to stop the pain, and dirt got into the cut.

15

20

Tasks

1. Study *lines 8–13*. Find TWO reasons why disease spread. Which of these is shown in **Source B**?

2. Study *lines 15–21*. Find FOUR ways doctors tried to cure sick people.

3. Why would the mother in **Source C** probably have died (see lines *22–24*) after she had had the baby?

4. Look at **Source A**. What would a woman think if she became sick in the Middle Ages?

Changes in medicine

Q

- Name TWO things that have changed since you were little.

- Why have they changed?

Things that did not change
Some things did NOT change in the Middle Ages. Doctors never found out what caused diseases.
5 Towns did not get cleaner.

Things that changed
But some things did change:

A. After 1200, the first hospitals were built. Nuns and monks
10 looked after the people.

B. Doctors tried new operations, with new metal tools.

C. After 1250, the English got new medicines from Muslim doctors.

15 **D.** After 1350, doctors began to cut up dead bodies to find how the body works.

One nun, called Elizabeth of Hungary, wanted to look after sick people. She drank the water they had been washed in, including the pus from the cuts on their bodies! In the Middle Ages, people thought this was good! When she died, the Pope made her a Saint.

Nuns looking after sick people in a hospital. How is it different to a modern hospital? ▽

SOURCE **A**

Task

Use the information in points **A–D** to explain how each of the following helped medicine to improve:

- monks and nuns,

- metal tools,

- Muslim doctors,

- cutting up dead bodies.

SOURCE B

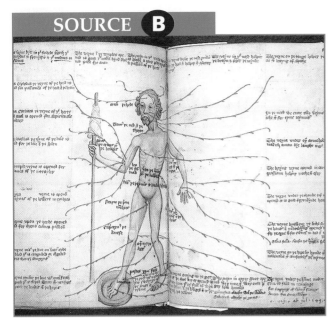

⚠ *A picture showing where doctors could cut sick people to take away 'bad' blood.*

Why things changed
Things changed because:

1. English traders met good Muslim doctors. 20

2. More people wanted to be monks and nuns.

3. Blacksmiths got better at making metal tools. 25

4. The Church lost some of its power (the Church had stopped doctors cutting up dead bodies).

SOURCE C

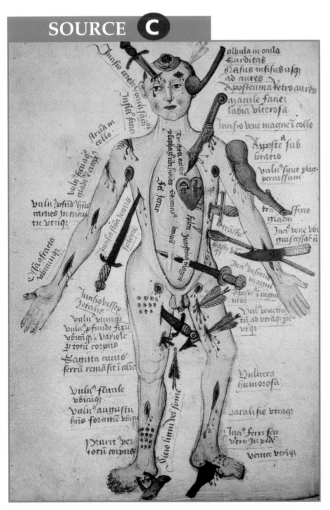

◄ *This picture shows wounds that doctors said they could cure in the Middle Ages. What wounds did they say they could cure?*

Tasks

1. How many times does the word 'doctor' appear on pages 50–51? Read the sentences and write down FOUR things about medieval doctors.

2. What did NOT change in the Middle Ages *(lines 2–5)*?

3. Look at the four **Things that changed** *(lines 7–17)*. Now look at **Why things changed** *(lines 18–28)*. Match up the causes to the four changes they caused.

The Black Death

◄ *This picture shows Death. He is killing people with his plague arrows. Look at the different people he is killing.*

Your Mission: *to investigate the Black Death.*

Take away all the dirt from the streets.

Keep London clean from all smells, so the smell will not cause any more deaths.

The smells poison the air, and make men sick.

▲ *A letter, written by King Edward III, in 1349.*

Q ● Have you ever been very ill?

● What did the doctors do to make you better?

The plague came to England on two ships. It came with the traders. The traders were sick – *they* brought it! They gave us the Black Death!
   People got lumps under their arms and
5 between their legs. Black lumps! They smelled bad. And how they hurt! People went mad. They cried out, and could not stop. After three days, they died.
   Plague! It killed young and old, rich and poor.
10 Nothing could stop it. Not the doctors – they ran away! Not the priests – they died saying their prayers. People said, 'This is the end of the world!'

In 1345, three planets came together in the sky.

   This caused the deaths . . . there was plague in the air.

NEW WORDS

ships, lumps, streets, planets, poison, whipped

This French doctor said that the planets caused the plague. ➤

SOURCE D

They gave me a bag. It had red and black poison in it. They told me to put the poison into the wells.

▲ *The French made this man say that the Jews had caused the plague. He said the Jews had poisoned the wells.*

Q Study **Sources B–F**. Find a source which matches these ideas about what caused the Black Death.

Cause of disease	Source
God	?
The planets	?
Bad smells	?
The Jews	?

SOURCE E

God lets bad plagues and wars happen. He uses them to punish people and to stop them doing bad things. The plague has come to England because many people were bad in their lives.

▲ *This was written by a monk in 1348.*

SOURCE F

▲ *Some people said God had sent the plague to punish them. To get God to take away the plague, they whipped themselves.*

Tasks

The plague came to England in 1348–50. Historians call it the Black Death. They learn about it by looking at what people wrote and painted at the time (**Sources A–F**). Imagine that you are a radio script editor.

1. Work with a partner. Choose a paragraph on page 52 (*lines 1–3, 4–8* or *9–13*). Read it out, as dramatically as you can.

2. Devise a radio script for two actors, pretending they live in the Middle Ages. The scene is set in 1349, when people are dying of the Black Death.

Make up a play in which the two people talk about why the plague has come, and what people should do about it.

3. Act out and/or tape record your play.

8 KINGDOMS AT WAR

IN THIS CHAPTER YOU WILL LEARN:

● **FOUR reasons England defeated Scotland, Wales and Ireland;**

● **THREE reasons England could not conquer Ireland and Scotland;**

● **EIGHT ways Owain tried to prove he was 'Prince of Wales'.**

NEW WORDS

independent: countries which **ruled** themselves.

invade

conquer

captured

Q What do the letters 'U.K.' stand for? Talk about places you have visited in the British Isles.

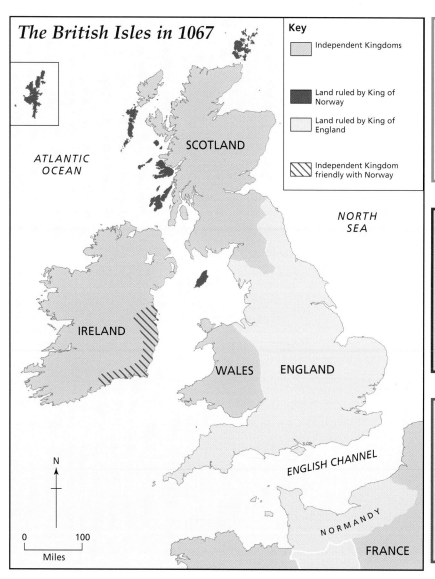

The British Isles in 1067

Key

Independent Kingdoms

Land ruled by King of Norway

Land ruled by King of England

Independent Kingdom friendly with Norway

ATLANTIC OCEAN

SCOTLAND

NORTH SEA

IRELAND

WALES   ENGLAND

ENGLISH CHANNEL

N

0   100
Miles

NORMANDY

FRANCE

Ireland

1171, King Henry II of Englan[d] invaded Ireland. Some Englis[h] lords went to live in Ireland.

Wales

1277 – 83, King Edward I of England conquered Wales. He built castles to control the country.

Scotland

1296 – 1328, the English trie[d] to conquer Scotland but wer[e] defeated. England agreed th[at] Scotland was an independen[t] country with its own king.

Tasks

1. Find and copy out the sentences with these words in them: 'conquered', 'wars', 'invaded' and 'controlled'.

2. Find TWO ways England in 1500 was different from England in 1067.

In the Middle Ages, England, Scotland, Wales and Ireland were independent countries. But England was bigger and richer. Over the years, England tried to conquer these other countries.

When King Edward I of England captured the wife and sisters of King Robert the Bruce of Scotland, he hung them in cages from the castle walls.

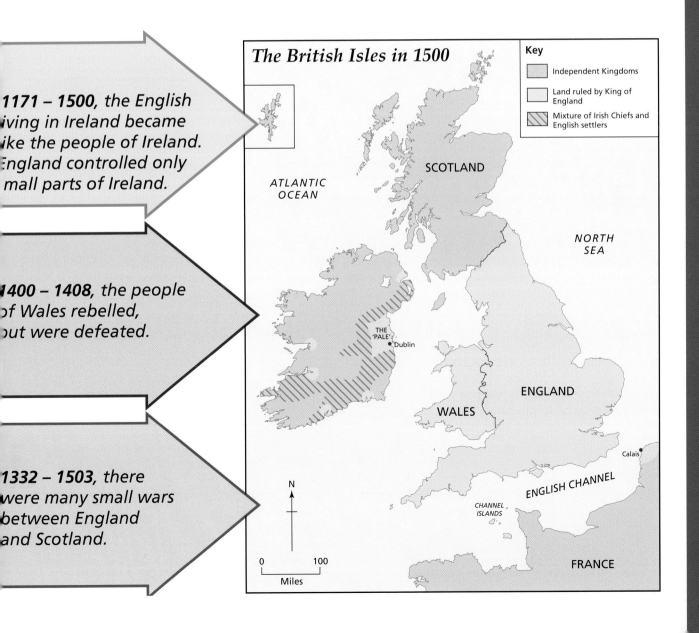

1171 – 1500, the English living in Ireland became like the people of Ireland. England controlled only small parts of Ireland.

1400 – 1408, the people of Wales rebelled, but were defeated.

1332 – 1503, there were many small wars between England and Scotland.

The British Isles in 1500

Key
- Independent Kingdoms
- Land ruled by King of England
- Mixture of Irish Chiefs and English settlers

ATLANTIC OCEAN

SCOTLAND

NORTH SEA

THE 'PALE'
• Dublin

ENGLAND

WALES

Calais •

ENGLISH CHANNEL

N

CHANNEL ISLANDS

0   100
Miles

FRANCE

Why was England powerful?

Your Mission: to find FOUR reasons why England was more powerful than Scotland, Wales and Ireland, and THREE reasons England failed to conquer Ireland and Scotland.

NEW WORDS

population: the number of people living in a country.

weapons

Scots

Irish

united

armies

compared to

SOURCE A

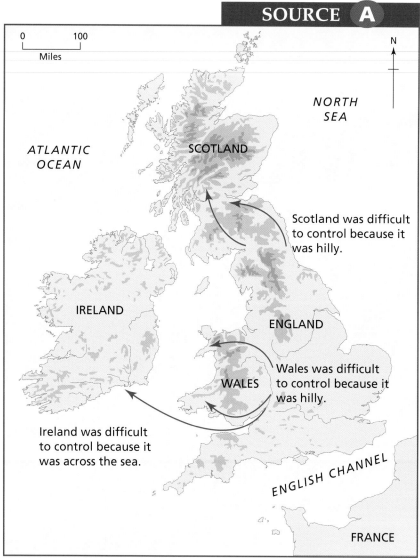

Scotland was difficult to control because it was hilly.

Wales was difficult to control because it was hilly.

Ireland was difficult to control because it was across the sea.

▲ England, Scotland, Wales and Ireland.

SOURCE B

1150	England	2½ million.
	Ireland	500,000
1250	England	4 million.
	Wales	300,000.
1300	England	5 million.
	Scotland	500,000.

▲ The population of England compared to Ireland, Wales and Scotland.

SOURCE C

The English defeated the Irish. They took land. They built castles.

They were able to win because they had better weapons.

But then they changed. They married Irish girls. They started to speak Irish.

In the end, they became 'more Irish than the Irish'.

▲ Written by a modern historian of Ireland.

INVESTIGATION

SOURCE D

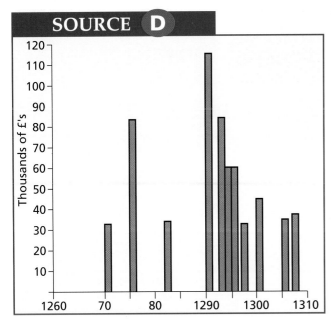

▲ *This shows how much the kings of England got in taxes, 1260–1310.*

The wool trade and the traders and merchants in the towns made England a very rich country.

The kings of England used this money to pay for big armies for their wars.

SOURCE E

In Wales and Ireland, the English faced many weak rulers who often went to war with each other.

They failed in Scotland because the Scots were united.

▲ *A modern historian.*

SOURCE F

The English could defeat the Scots.
The problem was – how could the king of England control Scotland from London, so far away?

▲ *A modern historian.*

Tasks

Copy and complete:

Why the English Defeated their Enemies

The English kings were able to win their wars because:

1. England had a bigger p_____ than Ireland, Wales and Scotland (**Source B**).

2. They had better w_____ than the Irish (**Source C**).

3. England was r_____ than Ireland, Wales and Scotland because of its t____ (**Source D**).

4. Wales and Ireland had w___ r_____ (**Source E**).

Why the English Failed in Scotland and Ireland

The English kings failed in Ireland and Scotland because:

1. In Ireland, the English b_____ like the Irish (**Source C**).

2. The Scots were u_____ (**Source E**).

3. Scotland was too f__ a___ from London to c_____ (**Source F**).

Owain Glyndwr – 'Prince of Wales'?

Your Mission: to investigate EIGHT things Owain Glyndwr did to prove he was the 'Prince of Wales'.

In 1283, Edward I, King of England, conquered Wales.   In 1303, he called his son the 'Prince of Wales'.   The Welsh people hated him.   In 1400, a Welsh lord named Owain led a rebellion.

5   Owain wanted to prove that he was the true 'Prince of Wales'.   He:

1. called himself the 'Prince of Wales';
2. said that there was an old story that he would rule Britain;
10 3. used the same coat-of-arms as the last Welsh Prince of Wales;
4. said he was descended from the first king of Britain;
5. lived like a king;
15 6. said that he loved war;
7. called Parliaments like a king, and
8. said he was descended from the old princes of Wales.

SOURCE B

He is of the family of the old princes of Wales.

▲ *Written by a Welshman, in about 1390.*

SOURCE A

> *The coat-of-arms of Owain from about 1409. Owain used the same coat-of-arms as the last Prince of Wales, who had been defeated by Edward I.*

SOURCE C

He is good in battle. He loves to ride war-horses.

▲ *Written by a Welshman in about 1400.*

SOURCE D

The first king of Britain was called Brutus.

Brutus had three sons. You are descended from his oldest son.

The great king Cadwalla was descended from Brutus, and I am descended from Cadwalla.

▲ *A letter from Owain to the king of Scotland in about 1402. He wanted the king of Scotland to help his rebellion.*

SOURCE E

Owain lived like a king with his men, even after he was defeated.

▲ *Written by a Welshman, some time after 1410. The writer liked Owain.*

SOURCE F

Owain has called a Parliament. Four men from every part of Wales have been told to go.

▲ *Written by a Englishman in 1405. He wanted to tell the king of England about what Owain was doing.*

SOURCE G

The only ruler of Wales . . . Owain, who God has made Prince of Wales.

▲ *This is what Owain called himself in 1400.*

SOURCE H

An old story says that three men will come, and that they will rule Britain.

We are those men, and we must work to make the story come true.

▲ *A letter written by Owain in 1405.*
He was writing to two powerful English lords who hated the king of England.
He wanted them to help his rebellion.

Tasks

1. On EIGHT slips of paper, copy the eight claims that Owain made to try to prove that he was the true 'Prince of Wales'.

2. Onto each slip of paper, write the source (**A–H**) which makes that claim.

3. Which do you think was Owain's BEST claim?

4. Use **Sources A–H** to put the correct date that Owain made each claim. Put the sources in date order – what was Owain's FIRST claim?

5. Design banners for Owain's army to carry into battle, showing all his claims to be the true 'Prince of Wales'.

9 WAR AND SOCIETY

IN THIS CHAPTER YOU WILL LEARN:

- EIGHT ways war affected people's lives;
- A speech from Shakespeare;
- FOUR battles of the Wars of the Roses;
- FOUR stages of the Battle of Bosworth.

NEW WORDS

affected

steal

armour: to protect the soldier.

mail: armour made from metal rings.

plate armour: armour made from sheets of metal.

sword

helm: a knight's helmet.

gloves, shield, lance

Today, we think that a good government is one which makes our life better.   In the Middle Ages, a 'good' king was one who could fight and win wars.

Task

Look back through this book.   Make a list of all the wars and battles you can find.

5 You must not think that people were fighting all the time in the Middle Ages.   But there were many wars, and the wars affected people's lives:

> English archers used 12,000 arrows at the Battle of Crecy in 1346.

SOURCE A

I have to work for the knight so he can fight for the king.

The king's wars cost a lot.   Parliament has become more powerful because the King has to ask it for money.

I got rich by stealing from my enemies.

The king gave me some land because I went to fight for him.

The soldiers burned down my house.

I could not trade in France because of the war.

I got rich selling weapons and food to the army.

All the fighting with France has made me love England!   And I hate people from other countries, such as France.

How War Changed
With all the wars, armies got much better:

10 **1.** At first, armies were made up of knights who were fighting because the king gave them their land.   Sometimes they were not very good soldiers!   This changed.   By 1350, the king used full-time soldiers to fight in his army.   They
15 were better soldiers.

2. Weapons got better.   After 1450, kings used cannons – which cost a lot of money.

Task

Compare the pictures of the Battle of Hastings (1066) on pages 4–5, with the picture of the Battle of Crecy (1346) on page 63.

3. Armour got better.   Look at Source B.   How did armour change in the Middle Ages?

Tasks

Look at **Source A**.

1. List EIGHT ways war affected people's lives.

2. Choose to be one of the people in **Source A**.   Memorise what 'you' are saying.   Ask your teacher to pretend to be the TV chat-show host of a programme called 'Should We Go To War?'

3. Choose and copy THREE important sentences from pages 60–61.

SOURCE B

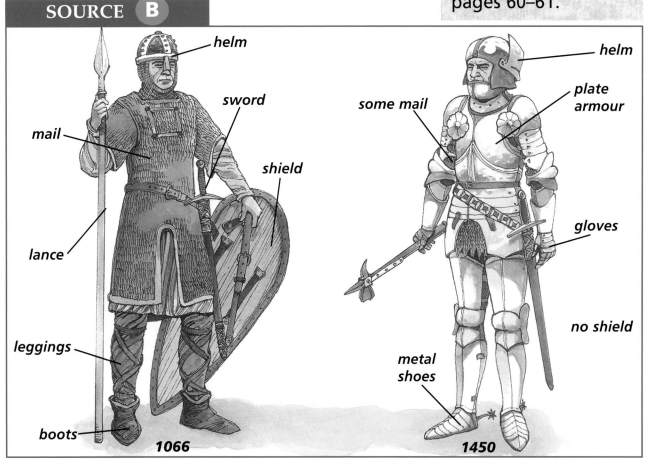

helm

sword

shield

mail

lance

leggings

boots

1066

helm

plate armour

some mail

gloves

no shield

metal shoes

1450

The Hundred Years War

Task

The passage below is a famous scene from Shakespeare's play, *Henry V*. Ask your teacher to read it to you.

Choose your favourite section, practise reading it, learn it, and then say it to the rest of the class, as bravely as you can.

NEW WORDS

born
witch
V: 5th.

[The scene: it is Saint Crispin's day, 24 October, 1415, just before the Battle of Agincourt. Henry V is at war with France. The French army has trapped him, and he is going to have to fight. As the scene opens, Henry's generals are saying that the French army is much bigger than the English army.]

GLOUCESTER: Where is the king?
BEDFORD: The king himself is rode to see their army.
WESTMORELAND: Of fighting men they have full sixty thousand.
5 **EXETER:** There's five to one; besides, they all are fresh.
SALISBURY: God help us! 'tis fearful odds.
    [Enter the KING]
KING HENRY V:
He who has no stomach to this fight,
10 let him go! We would not die in that man's company
that fears his fellowship to die with us.

Today is the feast of Saint Crispin.
He that outlives this day, and comes safe home,
will stand on tip-toe when the day is named,
15 and strip his sleeve and show his scars
and say: 'These wounds I had on Crispin's day.'

Old men forget: and all shall be forgot,
but we in it shall be remembered –
we few, we happy few, we band of brothers.

20 And gentlemen in England now a-bed
shall think themselves accursed they were not here,
and hold their manhood cheap while any speaks
that fought with us upon Saint Crispin's day.

Joan of Arc

She was born in 1412, at a time when England had conquered most of France.

In 1425, she heard voices telling her to go and fight the English.

The French soldiers loved her. She became their leader. She defeated the English army many times.

In 1430, she was captured. The English said she was a witch and burned her.

At the sea-battle of Sluys in 1340, many French soldiers were killed and fell into the sea. The English joked that the fish would be able to speak French!

The Hundred Years War

The 'Hundred Years War' was not a war that lasted 100 years! But *France* and *England* were at
5 war for 100 years.

The fighting started in 1337 because King *Edward III* of England wanted to be King of France.   He invaded France.   The
10 English won battles at *Crecy* (1346) and *Poitiers* (1356).   But Edward could not conquer all France, and slowly the French won back the land they had lost.

In 1415, King *Henry V* attacked   15 France again.   He defeated the French at the Battle of *Agincourt*, and conquered most of France. But Henry V died in 1422, and – led by *Joan of Arc* – the French   20 won back the land they had lost.

By 1453, the English had been defeated and they were pushed out of France.

SOURCE A

▲ *A picture showing English soldiers defeating the French at the battle of Crecy, 1346.*

Tasks

1. Read the passage on the Hundred Years' War on this page.   The most important words are in *italics*.   Choose FIVE words, draw a grid and make the words into a crossword.   Make up clues for the words. Give the crossword you have made to a friend to do.

2. Design a poster for an exhibition 'Joan of Arc: 600 years'.

The Wars of the Roses

In the years 1455–85, two powerful families – Lancaster, and York – tried to control England.   All the great lords helped one side or the other.   The badge of the Lancastrians was a red rose, and the badge of the Yorkists was a white rose, so the war was called 'the Wars of the Roses'.

NEW WORDS

families, badge, rose, Lancaster, Lancastrians, York, Yorkists, Tudor
IV: 4th.

The Wars of the Roses

1399   Henry of Lancaster took the throne from Richard II and became King Henry IV.

1422   Henry VI became king.   (He was mad).

1455   Battle of Saint Albans.   The Yorkists won. Richard of York took control of the government.

1460   Henry VI's wife killed Richard, and took back control.

1461   Battle of Towton. The Yorkists won.   Edward of York made himself king Edward IV.

1470   The Lancastrians put Henry VI back on the throne.

1471   Battle of Barnet. The Yorkists won.   Edward IV took back the throne. Henry VI was killed.

1483   Edward IV died.   His brother Richard of York became king Richard III.   Edward's two sons were killed.

1485   Battle of Bosworth – Henry Tudor defeated and killed Richard III, and became King.

THINKING IT THROUGH

64

What made them smile?

A Lancastrian   *A Yorkist*

Use the list of events on page 64 to find FOUR events that would have made the Lancastrian happy, and FOUR events that would have made the Yorkist happy.

● Explain your choices.

● Who had the last laugh?

SOURCE A

The Wars of the Roses were not bad, and they only lasted 30 years. There was only one year of real fighting. The battle of Towton was the only big battle. Not many people died in the fighting. Life went on pretty much as before.

▲ *Written by a modern historian.*

SOURCE B

The crown of England changed hands many times. But by 1500 all the Yorkist leaders were killed or in prison.
   The Tudors ruled England.

▲ *Written by a historian about the year 1500.*

SOURCE C

The great lords were ruined by the war they had started.

   But the Wars of the Roses hardly affected anyone else.

   Trade went on as before. Towns grew up.

▲ *Written by a modern historian.*

Tasks

1. Write the names of the FOUR battles of the Wars of the Roses onto FOUR pieces of card. Practise saying the names. Colour the card red if Henry Tudor won the battle. Leave it white if the Yorkists won. Muddle the cards up – then try to put them back in the right order.

2. Some historians say that 1485 marked the end of the Middle Ages in England. Read **Sources B** and **C** and explain why.

This is how Henry Tudor became King. In August 1485, Richard III was fighting for his throne. Against him was the army of
5 Henry Tudor, with 6,000 men.

Richard had more than 10,000 men, and another army was coming – 8,000 men led by Lord Stanley and his brother William Stanley.
10 Richard thought that Lord Stanley would help him.

Richard kept an army of about 2,000 men – led by the Earl of Northumberland – in reserve, to
15 help if something went wrong.

Maps 1–4 show what happened. Richard's main army attacked Henry Tudor's small army. Surely Richard was going to win!

Then Richard saw Henry Tudor 20 leave his men, and ride to William Stanley. Richard took 1,000 of his men and attacked Henry.

But Stanley did not attack Henry – he turned and attacked Richard. 25 And Northumberland did not come to help!

Richard was killed, and Henry Tudor became king.

Part 1

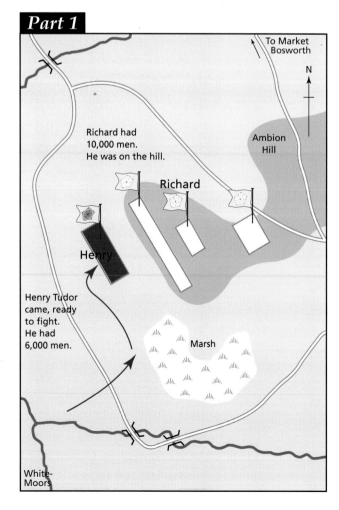

Part 2

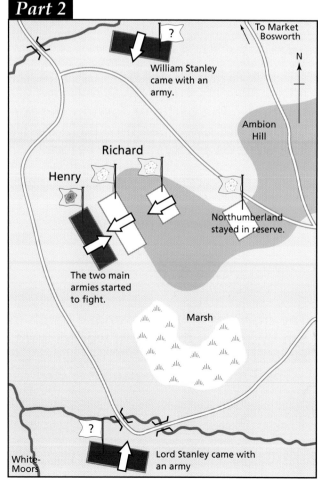

Tasks

1. Your brother has done a homework about the Battle of Bosworth, but it is all wrong! He has made 12 mistakes.   Can you find them?

The Battle of Bosworth took place on 1985. Richad (with 5,000 men) was fiting Henry Tudor (with 5,000 men).   Just then, an army of 6,000 men come, led by Lord Stalney and his bruther. Stanley helped Richard.   Richard was killed, and Northumberland became king.

2. You are a Yorkist, and you blame these people for the defeat at Bosworth:

Henry Tudor / William Stanley / Northumberland / Richard III

For each person, explain how they helped cause the defeat.   Who do you blame *most*!

Lord Stanley found Richard's crown in a thorn bush, and put it on Henry Tudor's head.

NEW WORDS

in reserve: kept out of the main battle, to help if needed.

Duke, Earl,

against, main

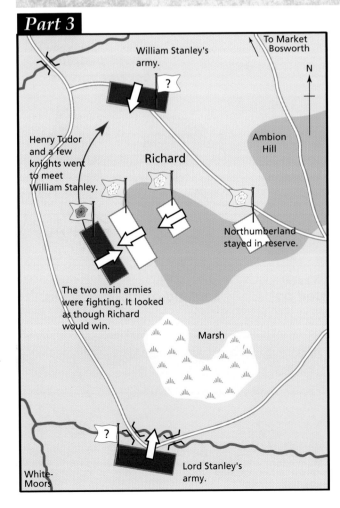

Part 3

William Stanley's army.

?

Henry Tudor and a few knights went to meet William Stanley.

Richard

To Market Bosworth

N

Ambion Hill

Northumberland stayed in reserve.

The two main armies were fighting. It looked as though Richard would win.

Marsh

?

White-Moors

Lord Stanley's army.

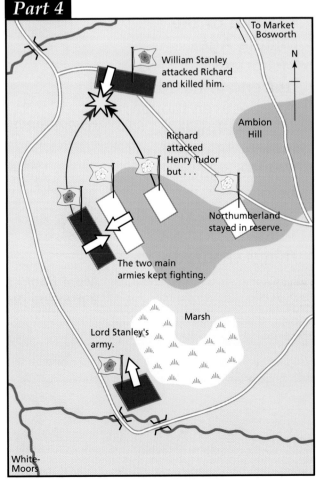

Part 4

William Stanley attacked Richard and killed him.

To Market Bosworth

N

Ambion Hill

Richard attacked Henry Tudor but . . .

Northumberland stayed in reserve.

The two main armies kept fighting.

Marsh

Lord Stanley's army.

White-Moors

10 WHERE HAVE WE BEEN? WHERE DO WE GO FROM HERE?

Change in the Middle Ages

Historians used to think that nothing
5 changed in the years 1066–1485. They called these years 'the Middle Ages' – the bad times of war and
10 plague in between the Roman Empire and modern times.

We know now that they were wrong.
15 Lots of things changed in the years 1066–1485.

The end of the Middle Ages

20 Historians call 1485 'the end of the Middle Ages' – even though, for most English people, life went on
25 just the same as before!

But in the years that followed, MANY things changed.

Changes 1066–1485

Different rulers.

More people.

More, bigger towns.

Fewer people became monks.

French lands lost.

More books (printed on a printing press).

England conquered Wales.

Parliament got more power.

Villeins got freedom.

Better doctors.

Where do we go after 1485?

What will happen to the Tudor kings?

Will people get richer?

NEW WORDS

Roman Empire

wrong

Printing press: monks no longer had to copy books by hand.

spoke

ruined

What will happen to the Church?

What will happen to Parliament?

Are there new worlds over the seas?

Tasks

Make a newspaper, called *'Medieval Times'*.

Look back through this book and choose stories to run under the following headlines:

'Our Greatest King'

'Our Worst Ruler'

'Biggest War Story'

'Worst Scandal'

'Biggest Disaster'

'Greatest Change'

'Daily Life'

'Church News'

'Health Page'

'Women's Page'

'A Place to Visit'

'Human Interest'.

Will the population keep growing?

Many farmers have become sheep farmers. Can they grow enough food?

Index

Tasks

1. Go through the list of 'People'. Can you remember what they were famous for? Look them up and see if you were right.

2. Go through the index entry 'Events'. Can you remember what happened? Look them up and see if you were right.

3. Go through the index entry 'Battles'. For each battle, find out when it was, who fought who, and who won.

4. Use the index to find out:

● when did Edward I tell all the **Jews** to leave England?
● which English king said he was overlord of **Scotland**?
● what six things did **Domesday Book** want to find out?
● what time did **Nuns** eat their main meal of the day?

5. Use the index to find out as much as you can about ONE of these:
  Barons, Women's life OR Traders.